The Horse Connection

Fred H. Cloninger

and

Armando R. Gonzalez

DEDICATION

This book is dedicated to all the hard working farriers for their understanding and skills, for their patience and resourcefulness, when taking care of one of nature's most amazing creatures.

Horses have been there for us throughout history,
not only for their endurance and agility,
but also for their companionship.

CONTENTS

A new day caring for one of God's most loved species

Preparing tools for work in cold weather

Tools of the trade

I am here
to fit you
with new shoes

Now,
let's see what
would be best
for you.

Molding shoe to horse's needs

Brother-Fred at work

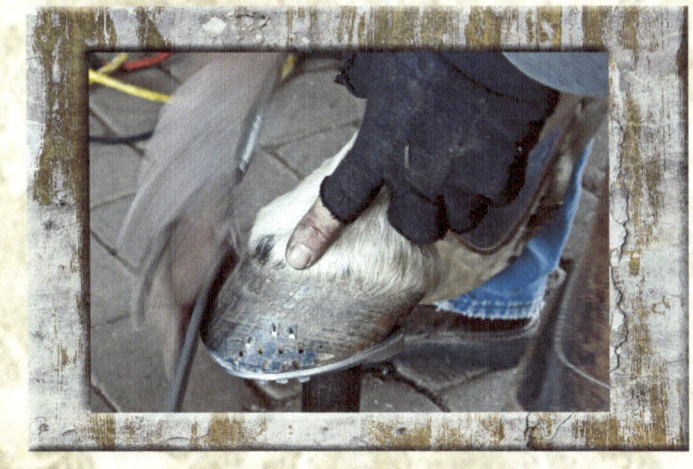

Done......

Another happy horse

.......Next!

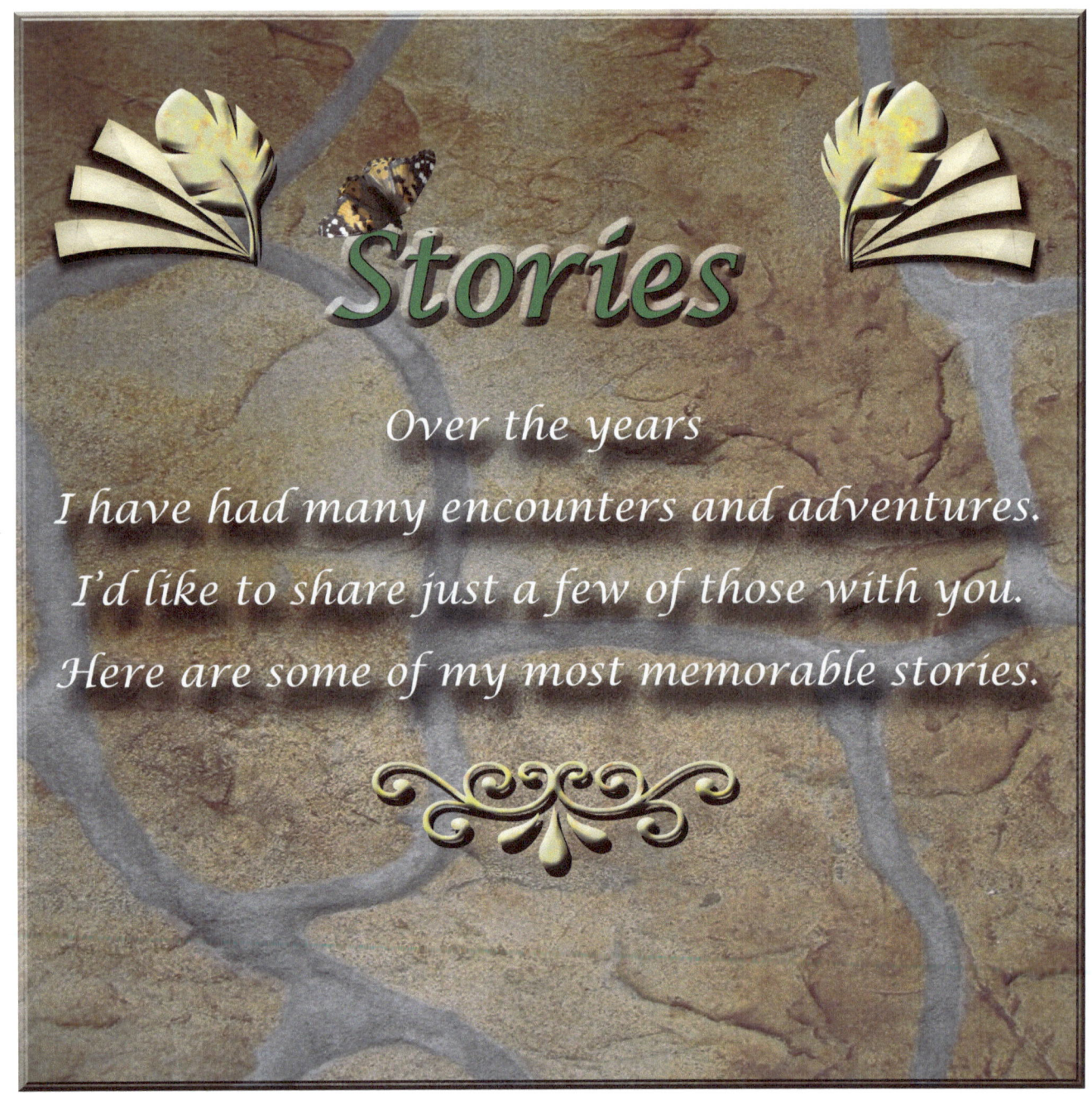

Stories

Over the years

I have had many encounters and adventures.

I'd like to share just a few of those with you.

Here are some of my most memorable stories.

I was around horses my whole life. My grandfather taught me how to touch animals.

People can give you that energy through their hand if you receive it.

He is the one that gave me the touch.

When I was young about four or five years-old, my grandfather had a walking horse.

A Farrier would come to my grandfather's farm and shoe his horse and I would study him intently.

I would watch him take a hot shoe from a fire, quench it in the water and shoe the horse.

I thought he was a god. I decided I wanted to be that man.

We had farriers that would come out and shoe our horses.

Later on, a friend would come out and shoe my horses for me.

He decided to give it up. So, when he did, I had to start figuring out how

I was going to shoe horses.

I didn't have a choice.

My neighbor up the road said he would help.

The first horse I shod was a mare.

Her name was Jitterbug.

I set the shoes and then I hammered the nails.

I must have done a pretty good job

because she actually could walk away.

I started to shoe a little more. People started talking. The next thing I knew people started calling. That was around 1989. In 1983 I lost my job working on the railroad. I went to Eastern School of Farrier in Martinsville VA in September 1989 and finished November of the same year. While I was there, I looked back on my life and thought about the man who I saw horseshoe my grandfather's horse when I was four years-old. I made him a handmade horseshoe and brought the shoe home for him in October 1989. I found out he was in a nursing home in Gastonia, NC. I went searching for him and found him in his room. I walked in the room with the shoe in my hand. I called his name.

He slowly sat up in the bed and fixed his eyes on me.

I said, "I got something for you."

He smiled, his eyes got bright.

I told him," I made this for you.

Don't let anyone get this shoe."

He informed,

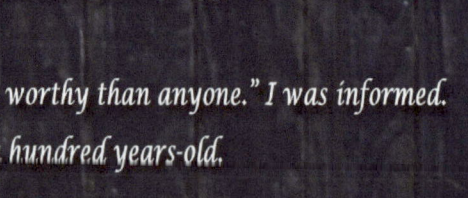

"Son, don't you fret, no one will get this shoe."

Later on that year, he died.

After he passed away, one of the family members brought me a pair of nippers

-that you use to cut the horse's hoofs.

"We would rather you have these because you are more worthy than anyone." I was informed.

They are a pair of Champion nippers. They are about a hundred years-old.

I still have them. They are priceless to me.

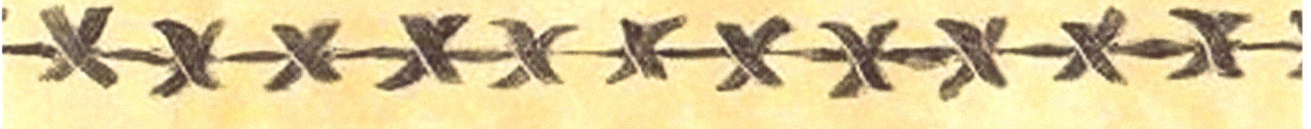

You never know what is going to happen during a day's work.
While I was shoeing a horse, I was talking with the horse's owner. I stated,
"As I have gotten older, I don't smell as good as I used to."
The horse's owner looked at me and replied," You're right.
You don't smell good." My head shot up in surprise, "That is not what I meant."
There was a paused silence between us and in a hushed voice
I heard the owner say, "You still don't smell good."

Most horses are like people.
They have doubt and they have fear.
The word fear means to me false expectations
that are not real.
Horses feel the energy of no fear
when I touch them.
When I touch horses, they feel the energy of calm,
quiet and peace.
Normally, on a good day with the horse,
it is just me and the horse.
When working with a horse, he has to trust me
to give me his foot.
Without his foot he cannot walk or run.
He has to trust me that I am going to give his foot back.
What's in your heart is in your hand.
The horse's heart is in my hand.
His heart is in his foot and his foot is in my hand.
Your horse has five hearts. A heart is in each hoof.
Blood pumps to each hoof.
Horses are more cat like than dog like.
A horse is next to a cat on the level of energy.
You have to be catlike. You don't manhandle a horse.
You ignore a horse like you would a cat.
What does it do? The horse comes to you.
When I first meet a horse with issues, I work with them.
The next time I see them, they are calm
because they trust me.

The term mare is used for a female horse.
One mare that I had was 'THE ONE'.
Her name was Charm and she was quite a mare.
She stood about 15.2 hands.
I got her as a four-year old.
We got along fine. She would die for me.
She was that kind of horse.
One year,
we decided to go to a horse camp in Missouri
and took 16 horses.
Out of three thousand horses in the camp,
a photographer took a picture of my horse
Charm and me.
One of the ladies at the camp told me to go
look at the picture of me and my mare.
It was really beautiful.
Four years later, her life ended too soon.
I was boarding horses at my barn.
One gray gelding was trotting into the barn
to go in the stall
when he suddenly turned around
back the way he had come from.
My horse had followed the gelding into the barn.
When she saw the gelding coming,
she slammed into the wall to miss the grey horse.
She died the next day.
...After she passed away a part of me died with her.

Pride

The horse I learned the most from was named "Pride". Pride was a two year old quarter-horse mare that my friend had bought. When I shoed it the first time, it went fine. He decided later that summer to sell the mare to a sixteen year-old boy. The teenager did not understand the horse at all and did not have any knowledge of horses in general, he asked me to shoe him, I said yes because I had shoed the mare before and it went fine. He brought the mare over to the barn, things were going fine until I reached for the back foot, it was the right hind, I set two nails in the shoe, I put the foot down and reached down to pick the left foot up.

She suddenly took her foot from my hand, brought it to her shoulder and kicked me in the chest.

She brought me to my knees, I had the imprint of the horseshoe in my skin and I couldn't breathe. I struggled to my feet and still couldn't breathe. I staggered to a refrigerator I had in the barn, opened the door, and stuck my head in it. The cold air hit my face and I took a breath. I told the young man, "I am going to finish shoeing the horse, I have two more horses coming from North Wilkesboro, NC. they are 60 miles away and I am going to shoe them too, you are going to stay with me until they get here, if you leave me and I die, I will haunt you" I informed him.

That was the day Pride got knocked out of me-- literally and I got knocked down a notch.

Brother-Fred's Writings

A few years ago,
I was going through a lot of personal turmoil.
To get me through the obstacles in my life,
I turned to writing.
Writing helped me get through the difficult time in my life.
I continue to write because I enjoy it.
I am happy to share it because it is also a part of me.

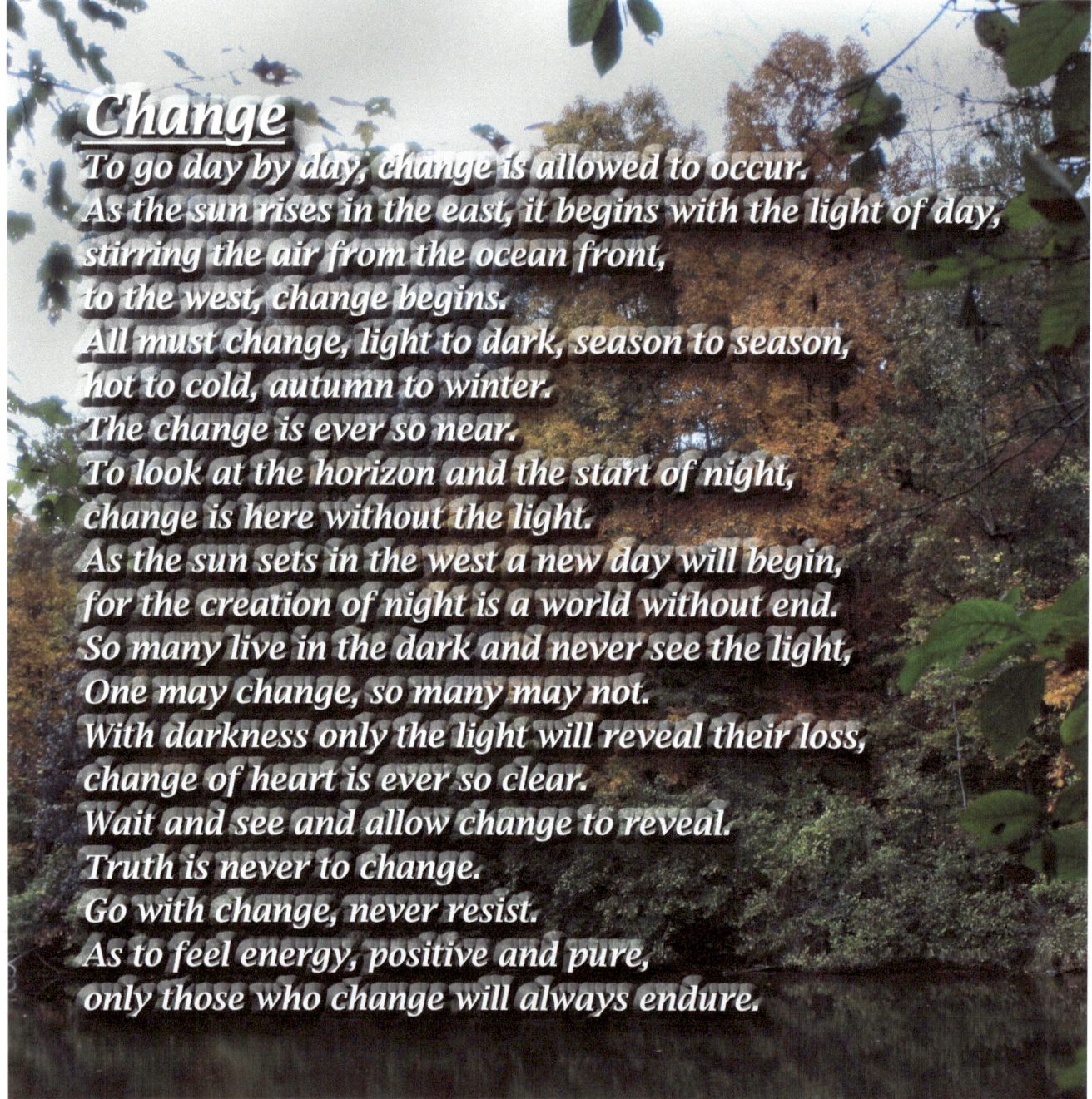

Change

To go day by day, change is allowed to occur.
As the sun rises in the east, it begins with the light of day,
stirring the air from the ocean front,
to the west, change begins.
All must change, light to dark, season to season,
hot to cold, autumn to winter.
The change is ever so near.
To look at the horizon and the start of night,
change is here without the light.
As the sun sets in the west a new day will begin,
for the creation of night is a world without end.
So many live in the dark and never see the light,
One may change, so many may not.
With darkness only the light will reveal their loss,
change of heart is ever so clear.
Wait and see and allow change to reveal.
Truth is never to change.
Go with change, never resist.
As to feel energy, positive and pure,
only those who change will always endure.

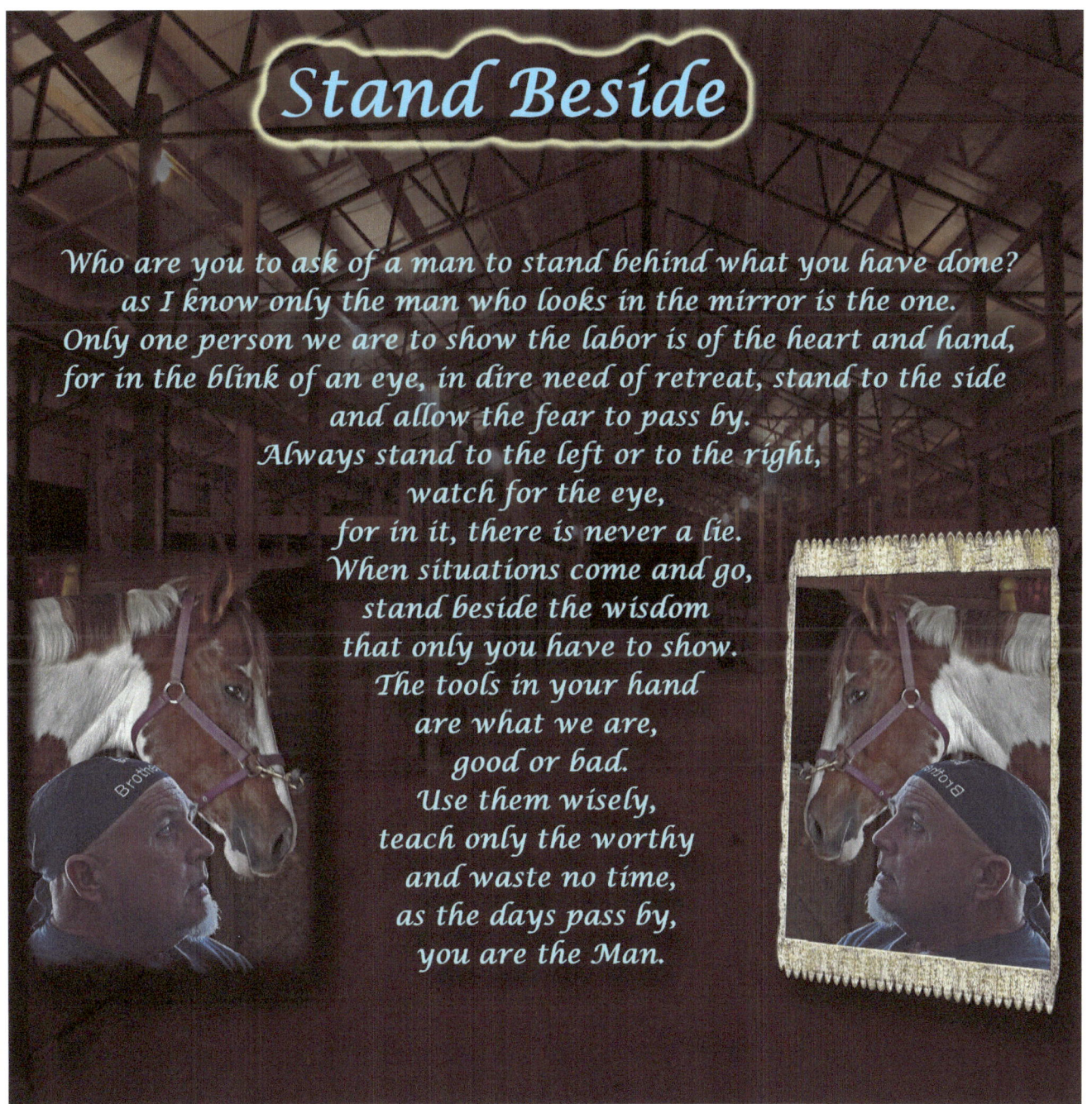

Stand Beside

Who are you to ask of a man to stand behind what you have done?
as I know only the man who looks in the mirror is the one.
Only one person we are to show the labor is of the heart and hand,
for in the blink of an eye, in dire need of retreat, stand to the side
and allow the fear to pass by.
Always stand to the left or to the right,
watch for the eye,
for in it, there is never a lie.
When situations come and go,
stand beside the wisdom
that only you have to show.
The tools in your hand
are what we are,
good or bad.
Use them wisely,
teach only the worthy
and waste no time,
as the days pass by,
you are the Man.

Treasure Chest

A vessel is a ship at sea, treasure chest inside with precious gold.

The heart is a vessel with treasures to hold,

one or two, or more, that are never to be told.

The vessel is strong and secure

to never share or speak what is under the lock.

For you have one key and only one heart.

Protect it dearly, no matter the cost.

The treasure belongs only to you.

Not about what others may say or sometimes do.

Protect the treasure that is only yours to have and to hold,

Never to be shared, nor ever to be told.

What is so important is we need to listen and be still,

Allow the heart to hold all the treasure and always conceal.

The Hand

The Cherokee Indian told me to give my hand and began to explain,
First finger was the prophet to prophecy;
Second was the teacher to teach the world;
Third was the preacher to preach throughout the land;
Fourth was the evangelist to go out in the world to speak the word;
Fifth was the Apostle – the Godly man.
All of the fingers came together as one awesome holy hand,
to show peace and love throughout the land.
With the touch he gave, I said,
 "The peace and love is shown in the outstretched hand,
  No harm will come to this holy man."
Many have been said to hear the word – listen and wait.
The second time you hear the same word,
memorize and repeat it to every man.
As I have now done with pen in hand.
Repeat and recite all that is to be.
Blessings and peace, Godly men always see.

Bird in My Hand

In the early morning on a spring day, the barn was alive with three horses standing,

Also a sparrow bird was alone with no second thought, not a word was spoken.

The owner of the horses entered and gathered the horses one at a time.

Trim and shod, on the last horse, the owner said, "Do not move." I asked why and then she said,

"Look down at your feet". And there it was a sparrow.

This moment was special for she knew nothing about the bird.

The sparrow came from 40 feet away to my feet.

As I reached down, my hand gently held the sparrow noticing the eyes were closed.

Touching the right eye, it opened and I said "My look," and then I touched the left eye and it also opened.

She spoke and said, "Give the sparrow to me." I replied, "What are you to do with the sparrow?"

She said, "A bird cage in my house will be a safe place."

Then I opened my right hand, and spoke to her, "Are you ready?" "Yes ," she replied. "Ok," I said.

And all in one moment the bird took wings and flew away.

The Nail

The Nail is a symbol.
The importance is not the nail,
but the marks left by the nail
on Jesus Christ's hands and feet.
The marks are the only man made
things that are in heaven.

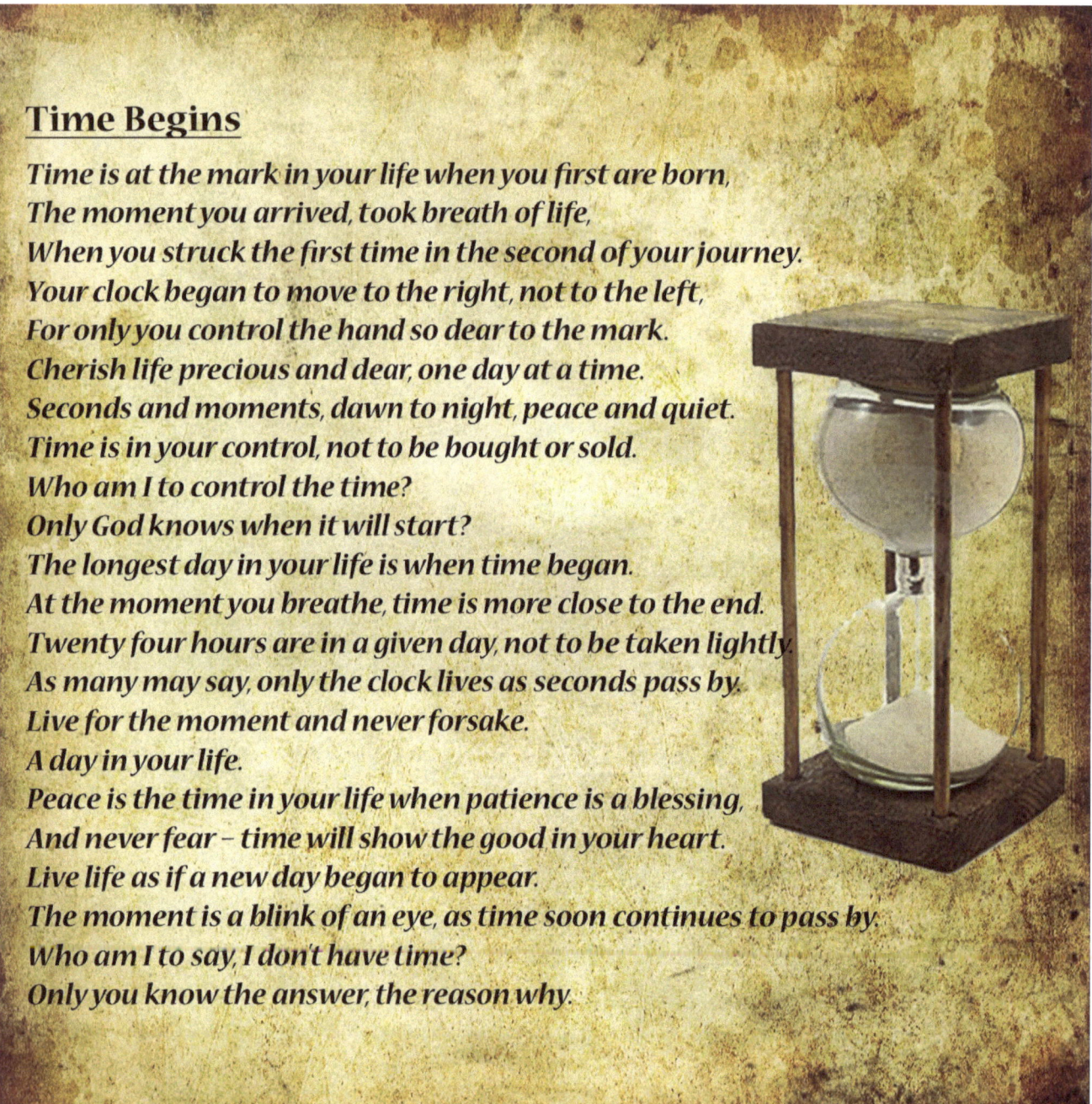

Time Begins

Time is at the mark in your life when you first are born,
The moment you arrived, took breath of life,
When you struck the first time in the second of your journey.
Your clock began to move to the right, not to the left,
For only you control the hand so dear to the mark.
Cherish life precious and dear, one day at a time.
Seconds and moments, dawn to night, peace and quiet.
Time is in your control, not to be bought or sold.
Who am I to control the time?
Only God knows when it will start?
The longest day in your life is when time began.
At the moment you breathe, time is more close to the end.
Twenty four hours are in a given day, not to be taken lightly.
As many may say, only the clock lives as seconds pass by.
Live for the moment and never forsake.
A day in your life.
Peace is the time in your life when patience is a blessing,
And never fear – time will show the good in your heart.
Live life as if a new day began to appear.
The moment is a blink of an eye, as time soon continues to pass by.
Who am I to say, I don't have time?
Only you know the answer, the reason why.

Fred H. Cloninger

Armando R. Gonzalez

The Book

*This started as an assignment for a
photography course, I chose Brother-Fred
as my subject because I felt his trade was
one many people were unfamiliar with.
I also felt that people were unaware
of the care and understanding that is
required to win a horse's trust.
I documented Fred's work, put a
picture book together and gave it
to him as thanks for allowing me to
document his work. Shortly after we
met Pam Wise and Steve Lawson
who brought their skills and guidance
to help make this project come together.
We added some very wise and thought
provoking writings by Brother-Fred
as the frosting ....all as if it was meant to be.*

*Thanks to all,
Andy Gonzalez*

The journey of my life was born again five years ago in a holistic blessing when I got involved with Healthy Stride.

Healthy Stride is an evaluation of horses balancing the posture and conformation.

Helping horsemen and horsewomen is the calling of this new skill.

Traveling this great nation has given me the most awesome experience of my career.

Helping other people excel is the acronym of Hope.

This has been the most incredible blessing of my life. Always have hope.   Never give up and finish strong.

Brother Fred-Cloninger

*I am a native of Colombia, South America and have lived in the United States since 1965.
After serving ten years in the Air Force I fell in love with and moved to North Carolina.
I have always been fascinated by photography and capturing nature
and events that otherwise would not have the opportunity to be appreciated.
I am grateful to have been involved in this project
and to have made the acquaintance of those connected with it.
Thanks to all for your help and encouragement.*

Armando R.Gonzalez